Family World

My Grandparents

Caryn Jenner

FRANKLIN WATTS
LONDON•SYDNEY

Sharing this book

This book shows the variety of roles that a grandparent plays in children's lives around the world. It provides a useful starting point to discuss how families everywhere are similar, but that each child's family is different and special.

• Remember that families are formed in different ways and grandparents can be step-grandparents, adoptive grandparents, foster grandparents or anyone else that a child thinks of as a grandparent.
• Sadly, many children experience the death of a grandparent. Like adults, children need to grieve. It may help them to make a memory box or scrapbook of things that remind them of their deceased grandparent.

Organisations for and about grandparents:
The Grandparents Association – www.grandparents-association.org.uk
Grandparents Plus – www.grandparentsplus.org.uk

First published in 2013 by Franklin Watts
Copyright © Franklin Watts 2013

Franklin Watts
338 Euston Road
London NW1 3BH

Franklin Watts Australia
Level 17/207 Kent Street
Sydney, NSW 2000

All rights reserved.

Series Editor: Sarah Peutrill
Series Design: Ruth Walton
Design: Maddox Philpot

Dewey number: 306.8'742
ISBN: 978 1 4451 1930 4
Printed in Malaysia

Franklin Watts is a division of Hachette Children's Books,
an Hachette UK company. www.hachette.co.uk

Please note: Some of the pictures in this book are posed
by models. All scenarios are fictitious and any similarities
to people, living or dead, are purely coincidental.

Picture credits: amorfati.art/Shutterstock: 4t. Yuri Arcurs/ Shutterstock: back cover. Asia Selects/Alamy: 13t. Atlaspix/Shutterstock: 7cl. auremar/Shutterstock: 7c. andreas balcazar/istockphoto: 14c. bikeriderlondon/Shutterstock: 23br. John Birdsall Photography/Photofusion: 18t. Blend Images/ Alamy: 16c. Blend Images/Shutterstock: 15t. Stephen Burres/ Shutterstock: 7t. c/Shutterstock: 12tl. Diego Cervo/Shutterstock: 23tl, 23tc, 23trl. Andy Dean Photography/Shutterstock: 23cr. Dinodia/Alamy: 5c. erdem/Shutterstock: 14t. Fancy/Alamy: 10t,19c. fatihhoca/istockphoto: 12b. fotoluminate/Shutterstock: 23cl. gabor /Shutterstock: 20-21. Globe Turner/Shutterstock: 5t, 6t, 8t, 9cl, 10c, 13tl, 17b, 18tr. granata1111/Shutterstock: 11t. Bartoz Hadyniak/istockphoto: 18b. herjna/Shutterstock: 9c. Image Source/Alamy: 11c, 13c. Imagine Asia/Alamy: 15c. javi indy/Shutterstock: 23ccl. Kamira/Shutterstock: 23bl. Nolte Lourens/Shutterstock: 10b. margusson/Shutterstock:9tr. Rob Marmion/Shutterstock: front cover. Megastocker/Shutterstock: 13cr. Mettus/Shutterstock: 23ccr. Monkey Business/Shutterstock: 8c, 12t, 23tcr. Orange Line Media/Shutterstock: 17c. Tim Pannell/Alamy: 6c. Jane September/Shutterstock: 4c. M. Shcherbyna/Shutterstock: 16t. Smile studio/Shutterstock: 7tr. Paul Stringer/Shutterstock: 10tr, 15tc, 15cl, 17t, 19t. Przemyslaw Szablowski/Shutterstock: 12c. Dana Ward/Shutterstock: 9t. Every attempt has been made to clear copyright. Should there be any inadvertent omission please apply to the publisher for rectification.

Contents

My grandparents and me

Your grandparents are your mum's parents and your dad's parents. All over the world, children like you have grandparents.

Ming and his sister, Li-Li, pose for a picture with their grandparents in China. They are the children's mum's parents.

In India, Ajay and Roshni's family celebrate their grandfather's 75th birthday.

These grandparents are their dad's parents.

Which of your grandparents are your mum's parents? Which are your dad's parents?

My grandmother

Your grandmother is your mum's mum or your dad's mum.

Angel's grandmother from Grenada tucks her in at bedtime. Angel calls her 'Grandma' or 'Granny'.

Lien's family is from Vietnam. She calls her grandmother 'Bà nôi'.

In France, Josette and Marie cook pancakes using their grandmother's old family recipe. They call her 'Grand-mère'.

What do you call your grandmother?

My grandfather

Your grandfather is your mum's dad or your dad's dad.

Lewis likes fishing with his grandfather in Australia. Lewis calls him 'Grandad' or 'Grandpa' or sometimes 'Gramps'.

In Afghanistan, Wasim calls his grandfather 'Neekah'.

Milana lives in Chile. She calls her grandfather 'Abuelo'.

What do you call your grandfather?

Living near

Some grandparents live near their grandchildren. Some even live with their grandchildren.

Arla's grandmother lives with her family in Norway. Arla tells her grandmother all about her day.

Tobi's grandmother lives in the same village in Cameroon. She often looks after Tobi.

In Spain, Hector and Maria live near their grandparents and see them almost every day.

? Do your grandparents live nearby? Do they help to look after you?

Living far

Some grandparents live far away.

Luka lives in Britain. He likes talking on the phone to his grandmother in Bulgaria.

When their grandfather comes to visit in Japan, Yoshi and his sister, Jun, meet him at the train station.

Rosie and Jack take a long flight on an airplane to visit their grandmother in New Zealand.

Where do your grandparents live? When was the last time you visited?

Having fun together

It's fun to spend time with your grandparents.

In Mexico, Felicia and her grandmother have races. Felicia rides her bike, while her grandmother zooms along in her wheelchair.

Emilio's family lives in Brazil. He and his grandfather love to play video games together.

Mali and Isra play a game called 'congkak' with their grandmother in Malaysia.

What do you do with your grandparents?

Family history

Grandparents often tell interesting stories about the past.

In the United States, Kristen and Zack look at family photos with their grandmother. They laugh at pictures of their dad as a little boy!

Dominic's grandfather grew up in Tunisia. Then he moved to Australia, where they live now. He shows Dominic these countries on the globe.

? Ask your grandparents about people and places in your family's past.

A special kind of love

All over the world, grandparents love their grandchildren in special ways.

Gabriel is from Nigeria. His grandfather is very patient when they read together.

Chandrika's family lives in Nepal. Her grandmother always makes time to play with her.

In Greenland, Malik's grandmother chats about all sorts of things while she teaches him to knit. Malik thinks his grandmother is very wise.

What are some special things about your grandparents?

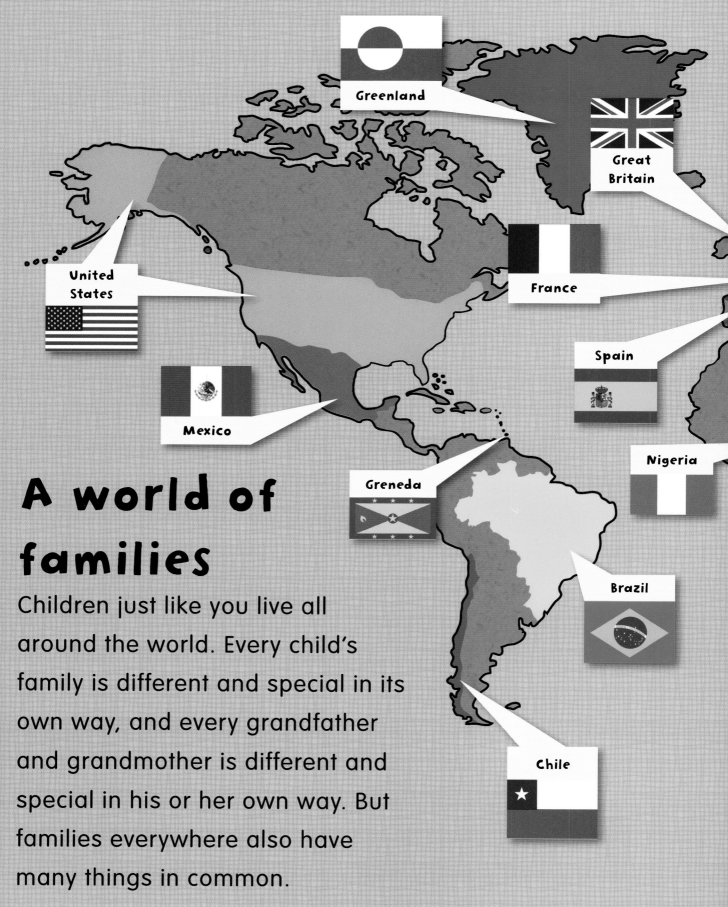

A world of families

Children just like you live all around the world. Every child's family is different and special in its own way, and every grandfather and grandmother is different and special in his or her own way. But families everywhere also have many things in common.

Greenland

Great Britain

United States

France

Spain

Mexico

Nigeria

Greneda

Brazil

Chile

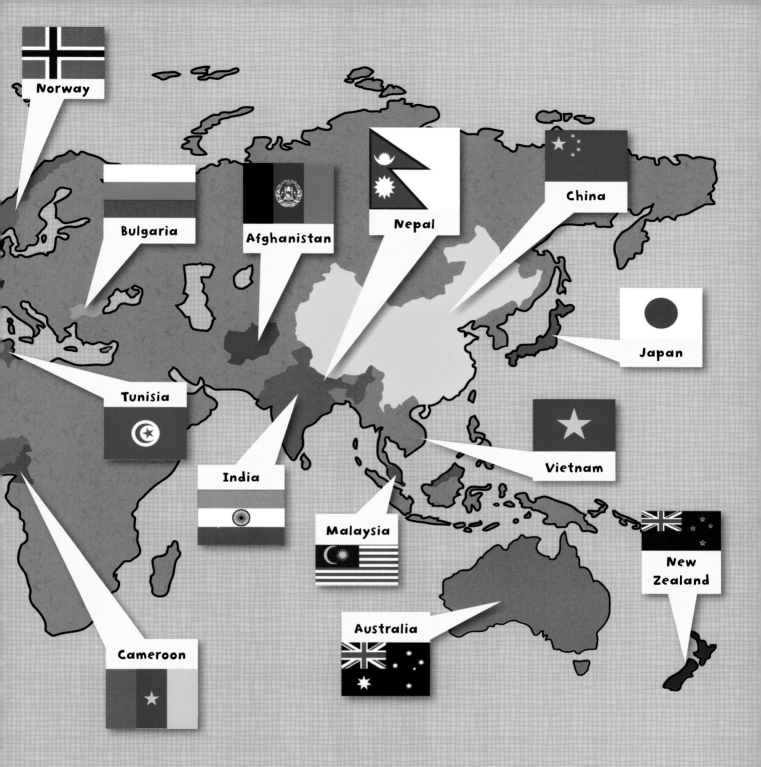

The families in this book live in the countries marked on this map. Can you find the flag that goes with each family in the book?

Activities

Make a certificate to tell your grandparents why they are special

Make an award certificate for them. Write 'I think you're special because…' or 'You're brilliant because…' and list the things they do that you think are special.

Find out how children around the world say 'grandmother' and 'grandfather'

Find out how to say grandmother and grandfather in different languages. Ask friends who speak other languages, or look it up in books or on the Internet. Here are a few languages to get you started:

Grandmother:
Norwegian – Bestemor
Chinese – Nai-nai
Swahili – Bibi

Grandfather:
Hindi – Dada
Portuguese – Avô
Japanese – Sofu

Ask your grandparents to share their memories with you

Look at photos with your grandparents and ask them to tell you about the pictures. Ask about when your grandparents were young. Where did they live? What was their school like? What were their favourite toys and games? What modern things hadn't been invented yet?

Make a family tree

A family tree shows the people in your family. Draw a picture of yourself and each person in your family, or use photos. On another sheet of paper, draw a tree. Stick your family pictures onto your tree. Your family tree can show the people you live with, or it can show lots of people in your family. You can even include your pets!

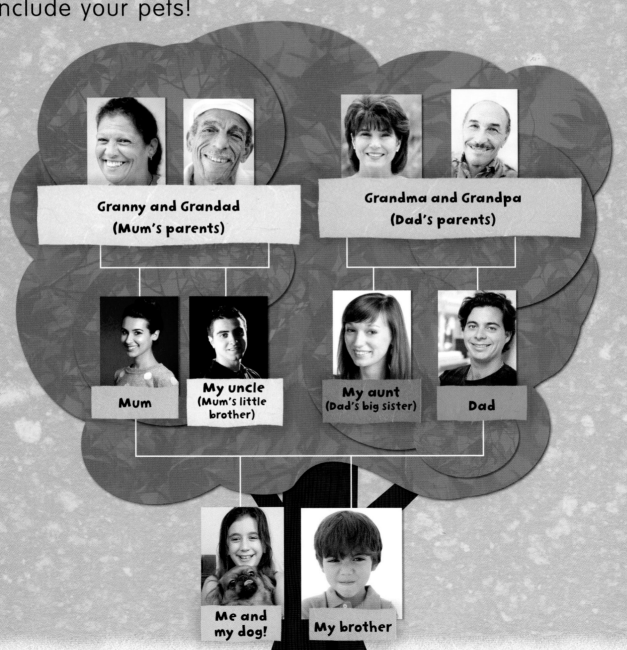

Granny and Grandad
(Mum's parents)

Grandma and Grandpa
(Dad's parents)

Mum

My uncle
(Mum's little brother)

My aunt
(Dad's big sister)

Dad

Me and
my dog!

My brother

Words about families

Here are some words you may use when talking about families.

Adopted – becoming part of a family that is not the family you were born into

Divorced – when parents split up and are no longer married

Family – a group of people who love and care for each other and are usually related

Foster mum or dad – grown-ups who look after you in their family if your parents can't

Grandparents – your mum and dad's parents

Half-brother or half-sister – a brother or sister who has the same mum or dad as you, but the other parent is different

Parents – your mum and dad

Siblings – brothers and sisters

Step-brother or step-sister – the son or daughter of your step-mum or step-dad

Step-mum or step-dad – if your parents are divorced and one of them marries again, the new wife or husband would be your step-mum or step-dad

Index